WINTERTIME
RHYMES

Edited by Daisy Job

First published in Great Britain in 2018 by:

 Young**Writers**

Young Writers
Remus House
Coltsfoot Drive
Peterborough
PE2 9BF
Telephone: 01733 890066
Website: www.youngwriters.co.uk

FOREWORD

Welcome to Let It Snow, a showcase for our nation's most brilliant young poets to share what they love most about winter and the festive season. From poems about Christmas and snow to drinking hot chocolate in front of the fire, this collection covers every aspect of wintertime.

Young Writers was established in 1991 to nurture creativity in our children and young adults, to give them an interest in poetry and an outlet to express themselves. Seeing their work in print will encourage them to keep writing as they grow and become our poets of tomorrow.

Selecting the poems has been challenging and immensely rewarding. The effort and imagination invested by these young writers makes their poems a pleasure to enjoy reading time and time again. I hope you enjoy reading them as much as we did.

CONTENTS

Buckler's Mead Academy, Yeovil

Jennifer Morgan (12)	69
Alisha Wilde (12)	70
Keira Stevenson (12)	72
Keegan Bond (12)	73
Cody Isaacs (12)	74
Jamie-Leigh Rose (11)	75
Hannah Beedle (13)	76
Carrie Jackson (12)	77
Ellie-Mai Lauchlan (11)	78
Jessica Pitman (12)	79
Ellie Kirkpatrick (13)	80
Christian Hobson (12)	81
Madison Dummer (12)	82

Carrickfergus College, Carrickfergus

April McGookin (13)	83
Kate Neill (14)	84
Niamh Alexander (13)	86
Matthew Ashe (13)	88
Casey Holmes (14)	90
Joshua Miller (14)	91
Oliver Boyce (14)	92
Tony Yordanov (14)	93
Stephen Gould (14)	94
Aaron McCalmont (14)	95

Harris Academy, Morden

Yaana Seewoolall (12)	96
Ida Paradowska (13)	97
Voichita Bura	98

King James' School, Almondbury

Thomas Prewett (11)	99
Beata Anna Palasz (11)	100
Amelia Kate Chaplin	102
Brook Seed (11)	103
Beckie Hodge (11)	104
Grace Throssell (12)	105
Benjamin Robert Copley (11)	106

Morgan John Kirk (12)	107

La Scuola Italiana A Londra, London

Laura Gancia (7)	108
Julia Alice Pensa (10)	110
Federica Collavo (9)	111
Tommaso Lombardo (8)	112
Edoardo Pallotti (8)	113
Caterina Annabelle Berg (9)	114
Eleonora Terranova (6)	115
Michele Pediconi (8)	116
Camilla Moni (9)	117
Clotilde Paino (7)	118
Aurora Pandolfi (8)	119
Samuele Lombardo (11)	120
Sofia Visona (8)	121
Tommaso Sartore (9)	122
Emma Terranova (8)	123
Elena Chionsini (9) & Carlo	124
Henry Jackson-Proes (9)	125
Vittoria Ginevra Vendramin Giardina (7)	126
William Ian Berg (6)	127
Virginia Elisabetta Vendramin Giardina (5)	128
Massimo Buccollato (6)	129
Joss Monachello (8)	130
Tommaso Busco (9)	131
Lucrezia Leone (10)	132
Greta Forestali (8)	133
Ettore Moni (7)	134
Giorgia Rinaldo (6)	135

Teesside High School, Eaglescliffe

Georgia Pallister (14)	136
Mazie Mae McKenna (13)	137
Imogen Hall (12)	138
Ruby June Rennison (12)	139
William Riley (13)	140
Phoebe Croft (12)	141

Isabelle Blackburn (12)   142
Emily Carney (12)   143
Ella Poulton (12)   144
Amelia Hall (12)   145
Ruby Liddle (13)   146
Melanie Dailey (13)   147
Phoebe Dailey (13)   148
Dominique Moore (12)   149
Harrison Murphy (12)   150
Marcus Keenan (13)   151

The Crypt School, Gloucester

Benjamin Lovell (12)   152
Jack David Boucher (12)   154
William Tidmarsh (12)   156
Louis Powles (12)   157
Jack Pryor (12) & Josh   158
William Robinson (12) & Uzair   159
Jacob Taylor (12)   160
Cameron Frederick (13) & Zac   161
Oliver Dove (12) & Abdur-   162
Rahman
Felix Baldwin (13)   163
Thomas Usmar (12)   164

THE
POEMS

Let It Snow

One snowy night, a little girl and her dad went out sledging,
So off they went through the trees and walls of stone.
Then they made it by the frosty hillside.
The little girl was very nervous at first
But she was brave and started going up the merry white hill.
When they both made it to the top
They popped down the sledge, *klonck!*
She went on the front and her dad went on the back.
Off they went, "Weeee!"

She jumped off the sledge and suddenly felt a shiver.
She laughed, rolling down the snow.
That was fun, she made her way to the top
And saw another girl called Steph,
They said, "Hi," and went back down, woohoo!

Shivering, bravely she hopped on the minty green sledge
While her dad was pulling it to take her home.
Finally, they were home where they enjoyed hot chocolate
And the warmth of the fireplace.
Hugging in the fluffy blankets
They shared family Christmas stories
Followed by a hot roast dinner.

Evie Harwood (9)

Winter Wonderland

My winter wonderland,
A weather of magic,
All twisting into a swirl of snow,
As the fireworks begin to fade,
And the blossoms begin to drift down,
You must know,
That the delight of a frosting season,
Is coming to the end of a night,
When will my winter wonderland arrive?

The one wish I had used
Is now into the mist,
Floating into what seemed like a mystical blur,
Away, away,
Into the depths of a haze,
While the clouds scatter out the snow,
Soon landing into a puddle of white,
When will my winter wonderland arrive?

The fire dances in the light,
In its freedom,
When the thunderstorms strangle the land,
Which was covered in a sparkling dreamland,
Crunching underneath the footprints of the people,
Still, silent and calm,

Just like the breeze,
But with the lit forest floor,
When will my winter wonderland arrive?

An eerie silence echoes,
Through the hollow of the tree,
One knew not how to open,
Because the magic within
Is so powerful,
That the stars in the midnight sky,
Lay untouched,
When will my winter wonderland arrive?

Upon the blurred lights,
Sat the man in the moon,
Who overlooked,
Each and every seven seas,
But my wishing star,
Just keeps on shooting forwards,
Forwards into the whistling winds,
As the snowflakes whisk into a finger of the branches,
So... when will my winter wonderland arrive?

Sehrish Malik (10)

Winter Is My Best Season

How I love this beautiful season,
When the days get colder, for one reason.
Winter is here, much to our delight,
For we can have a snowy view, even at night.
The roofs are covered with sheets of snowy white,
And so are the cars that are gleaming with light.

Although the adults complain that it's cold,
Us kids object, for winter's as good as gold.
We put on our coats and run outside,
With smiles on our faces and arms spread wide.
Shaping snowballs and building snowmen (oh what fun),
We also build our own snowy den.

We begin our epic snowball fight most excitedly,
Throwing snowballs and dodging them swiftly.
We have the best snowball battle,
And reward ourselves with an apple.
After a while, we have tea in our den,
An awesome day that we rate ten out of ten!

So why is winter the best season?
Oh, there's too many a reason.
Snow beautifies our houses with its white sheets,
And allows us to play with the snow,
Shaping them like sweets.

Winter makes us do some sledging
And the building of snowmen,
To have snowball fights and have tea in our den!

Hafsah Saleem (11)

Happy Christmas Times

It was nearly Christmas time
Time to get a nice, green Christmas tree.
It was a really, crazy time to spend.
In the morning, when I woke up
I looked up to the window
And I saw that everything was covered in white fluffy snow.
I got down to the living room
And everyone in my family was talking happily,
With big smiles on their faces,
Standing near to the fireplace.
After, Mum brought me my breakfast.
I asked my mum, "Can I go outside to play with snow?"
She said, "Yes of course.
We are going with you to make a great snowman
And play with snowballs."
When we were outdoors we saw so much snow all around.
This made me so joyful
While it was still snowing.
The birds were singing happy carols
And they were flying all around in joy.
As it's wintertime, all animals were getting more sleepy,
And getting ready for hibernation
From cold, to find somewhere else to go and find a good
warm place.

The trees were losing their leaves
And even some of them haven't got any now
They still looked amazing
And brightly sparkled the snow.

Dariusz Slysz (10)

Hark! Hark! Hark!

On a cold winter's night, silent as it snows.
Hark, hark, hark, let it snow!
Snowy mountains and valleys.
Hark, hark, hark, let it snow!
Children are playing, making snowballs.
Hark, hark, hark, let it snow!

Children having snowball fights.
Hark, hark, hark, let it snow!
Making a snowman is a delight and fun.
Hark, hark, hark, let it snow!
Angels in the snow are alright and mild.
Hark, hark, hark, let it snow!

The skies are star bright, star light.
Hark, hark, hark, let it snow!
The trees are white,
There is snow in the air.
Hark, hark, hark, let it snow!

Snow is falling and it's crystal-white.
Hark, hark, hark, let it snow!
The roads are all icy and slippery.
Hark, hark, hark, let it snow!
School being cancelled is the talk of the town.
Hark, hark, hark, let it snow!

Coming in from the cold I sit in a rocking chair.
Hark, hark, hark, let it snow!
A cup of hot chocolate and marshmallows I behold.
Hark, hark, hark, let it snow!
To the fireplace I will rest my feet.
Hark, hark, hark, let it snow!

Brian Delali Tsikata (9)

Waiting For Winter!

As winter approaches, signs of autumn start to fade,
Arrangements for Christmas are constantly being made.

I walk into warmth after a cold winter walk,
As my teeth chattered, I am trying to talk.

Outside icicles are hiding from the cold,
Indoors, old festive tales are being retold.

Snow hasn't arrived here yet, but it can't be long,
Men are cutting logs, they've got to be strong!

I love choosing a Christmas tree,
There are so many different sizes to see!

All the decorations are hung up proud,
Carol singers come and sing out loud.

Oh, what fun we are having!
It's so nice to see all my family laughing!
I love winter, I bet you do too.
The best bit for me is playing with presents,
The ones that are exciting and new.

Unfortunately winter can't last all year,
It comes then goes, leaving a tear.
Not everything is bad though,
Spring flowers are starting to grow.

Isabel Arrowsmith (12)

A Winter Wonderland Dream

My winter wonderland is filled with snow,
with naked trees and gleaming lamp posts;
all in sync and flow.
So, let it snow...
Not too distant, I see the beaming moon
amidst the glistening stars,
whilst romanticising the beauty which surrounds me,
but ignoring the 'zooming' cars.
Many footprints are continuously left behind,
as I stroll across the bridge,
even though I feel like I'm sitting in a fridge.
So, let it snow, more...
Beneath the bridge,
the ravishing river carries the moon's reflection,
and the dazzling azure of the undulating waves
embrace it with affection.
One cannot get enough of the cold yet refreshing air,
because the wind kisses the soul tender with care.
So, let it snow, even more and more...
But the best sight is glaring upon the snow
melting on the skin, as soon as it touches me,
my heart dances with ecstasy
and jumps up and down from the waist to the chin!

Laraib Samar (14)

Kittens In The Snow

Snowflakes settling on the windows
like stars made out of snow
and children gathering up what's left
ready to build and throw

They run to get their mittens on
and leave the roaring fire
and into the cold they go once more
as my kittens and I retire

The flames dance and warm our fur
and we spread out our paws to nap
and the open doors bring in the cold
what a wonder it is to a cat

As all children do, the kittens run to play
and I follow cautiously to make sure they don't stray
my warm soft paws grow icy when they hit the snow
I stand there watching and decide to follow

What fun this curious stuff is
oh, how I wish it could never end
but the sun will soon come
and the winter will bend

We play all day
jumping and crashing around the snow
but now we know the fun it is we don't want to go
and later we dream for tomorrow to bring more joy

My last wish for the year is
let the wonder continue
and the joy stay here
for nature to let it snow.

Amber McLoughlin (14)

Winter Wonderland

It never snowed before,
What a beautiful sight,
More than you could describe.

Am I Alice?
Can I see a talking rabbit?
Do I fall down in a hole?
Because I'm feeling like it's...
Winter Wonderland.

We have a party,
It will last till the snow stops!
It's hard to see when it stops because...
This seems to be going on forever.

Am I Alice?
Can I see a talking rabbit?
Do I fall down a hole?
Because I'm feeling like it's...
Winter Wonderland.

I love snowmen,
But you know what's even greater?
A snow dog!
Is it my imagination?

Because I'm feeling like I saw a...
Snow dog!
Walking fast to a hole in a tree,
Calling my name; Bee.
I fall down a hole, there was a bottle
Which had snow that said, "Eat me!"

A few hours later I opened a door
To my astonishment
My dream...
A winter wonderland!

Jerusalem Amaeshi (11)

Winter Fun

It's November and winter is near
I've been waiting for this time of year
For Christmas, New Year,
And the fun you can have in the snow
And the wind that turns into a chilling blow

The trees are bare without any leaves
And some animals have stopped acting as thieves
As it is time for them to hibernate
And prepare for a long sleep before it's too late

Every child is excited for the night of Christmas Eve
As tomorrow there is a gift for each child to receive
From Santa who rides on his sleigh in the snow
And one of his famous sayings are, 'Ho ho ho!'

When you wake up in the morning there is a chill outside
It's so frosty that you'll slip and slide
A white blanket is placed on the grass at night
And in the morning it's a sparkling sight

Winter is a time for everyone to enjoy
Whether you like playing outside or inside with a toy
It's also a time to celebrate with your family and friends
Because in winter, the fun never ends!

Bhoomija Singh (11)

Winter Wonderland

W inter's divine resplendent ice chateau is competently made from ice and snow.

I nside the exquisite chateau, the florid, lustrous light never goes.

N ever do the malicious spirits pass.

T he blanket of penetrating snow is all over the grass.

E very intriguing animal from day to night

R olling in the frigid snow until they're out of sight.

W owed by the repulsive ice queen's power

O ceania's flag waving in the immense tower.

N umerous people in this glacial place

D on't have any choice but they get blasted to illustrious space.

E ating distasteful, macabre stone-cold meals,

R evolting roasted seals

L ots of impeccable, amicable, affectionate people inside

A rctic air blowing outside

N ative in winter wonderland

D uring diverting parties, wine is banned.

Fathemi Syeda Jannat (8)

Let It Snow!

Here comes the big freeze!
"A snow day at last!" the children shout.
Eagerly grabbing their coats, before heading out,
Sledges, snowmen and snowballs galore,
The children are so excited to explore...
The fluffy white blanket covering the grass,
Off they run, making footprints at last.
Hours they spend, playing in the thick, fluffy snow.
But then came the rain, oh no!
Inside they run, as fast as they can.
Once warm indoors, they stare back at their snowman.
Watching him melt, as the rain pelts,
The look of dismay, their mother has felt.
Off to the kitchen she heads,
Then giving the children a shout.
Holding mugs of hot chocolate,
Marshmallows topped with sprinkles.
The children are sat in their cosy quilt, round the fire,
Watching the Christmas lights as they twinkle!

Amber Kaur Sury (10)

December Delights

Snowflakes as soft as cotton wool
Gently parachute from the sky,
Blanketing the naked trees
As they gracefully tumble by.
A tingle in my fingers
And numbness in my face,
They remind me of the unfortunate risks
That accompany such grace.
Icy air whistles through my ears
Just like pipers piping
Or like the sound of bells
On the reindeer Santa will be riding.
Cheerful children's faces light up
As bright as a Christmas tree
When they open a present that they love,
Or indulge in delicious turkey.
With the scent of pine and cinnamon
Slipping through my nose,
I can smile as brightly as the sun
Whilst I am warmed by my woolly clothes.
The joyful grins my siblings wear
Cease to disappear.
There is a sense of serenity in the air,
Winter is finally here.

Alicia Hassiakos (15)

Spend Christmas Together

Christmas is best with family around
Everyone smiling, not one with a frown
Families putting up Christmas trees
Whilst friends throw snowballs in the snowy breeze
Making memories to remember forever
Don't forget, spend Christmas together.

Christmas lights as bright as can be
People in unison, singing with glee
Drinking hot cocoa and eating mince pies
Watching the stars in the cold, night sky
Making snowmen in the snowy weather
Don't forget, spend Christmas together.

Remember, show love and joy at this time of year
And don't forget to spend Christmas cheer
So this Christmas, whatever the weather
Don't forget, spend Christmas together!

Erin Kennedy (12)

My Favourite Time Of The Year

Hat, scarf, gloves and wellies are all on ready.
The sweet smell of snow hits you.
Icicles dazzle like diamonds in the daylight.
Sledging, snowmen and snowball fights
Are the highlights to my life.

Snowflakes glide graceful from the sky, kiss our cheeks
And make everything shimmer, sparkle and shine.
The white wintery wonderland covers the trees
Almost as if it is there to please.

Onesies on, fire roaring, hot chocolate is boiling.
Snuggled up warm, waiting for Home Alone to come on.
Tiny droplets of magic began to fall
Each one more mesmerising than them all.

Family together.
Having the best time ever,
I wish this could last forever.

Olivia Gladders (15)

Winter Is Here

I step outside,
My smile grows wide,
For winter is my favourite season,
Here's each and every reason;

I look up, the sun is glowing,
I look down, it's been snowing,
I'm wrapped up warm, so don't worry,
Although there could be a snow storm, I'd better hurry.

And though it's a winter's night, the sun still does beam,
From our faces it would seem,
Drinking hot chocolate with marshmallows and cream,
In this moment, life feels like a dream.

Dressing up the Christmas tree
Fills me with glee,
Going to parties is really sublime,
With my family and friends I have such a great time.

Winter has only just begun,
But I can already feel the joy and the fun.

Erin Howat (14)

Waiting For The Snow To Go!

I crawl into my tree house bed.
I stay at home so I don't get wet.
Outside my house is where cruelty lies.
The snow and ice won't let me thrive.
All the humans play in the snow,
But I don't because it makes me cold!
There are no animals so you can't play.
There are no animals because they don't want to stay.
I'm a bird that only sings,
I'm a bird that needs spring.
All the snowflakes swirling around,
It makes me dizzy so I will fall to the ground!
I am counting down until it's spring,
I can't wait until the new season begins.

Taybah Saba Choudhury (9)

Autumn To Winter

Autumn and winter are fighting a battle,
Both trying to own the next season,
But when the misty nights start drawing in,
We all know that winter will win.

She freezes our water,
Bites at our fingers,
But all through the season, autumn still lingers.

Our ponds are frozen,
The ground is cold and hard.

Winter seems quite bleak
Until snow starts to fall.
I watch it in those winter nights,
Wrapped up in my warm shawl
And see the magic of winter settling in.

The world is frozen to its core,
Until winter is here no more.

Ellen Leila Jones (11)

It's That Time

When the first snowflake falls,
I know it's time to deck the halls.
We all become sedentary,
While everything remains merry.
The snow outside is Arctic white,
Everyone gazes at the sight.
All the kids have a snowball fight,
Then walk home with a little frostbite.
Our Christmas tree is overflowing
And everyone has their good side showing.
We breathe the scent of gingerbread,
Before I crawl into my bed.
Dad reads a story about the North Pole,
While I hope I don't get coal.
Mum gives me a kiss goodnight,
Before I snuggle close and tight.

Zoë Grainne O'Hare (11)

Christmas, Smifftmas

Let me introduce you to my cat,
His name is Smifftmas
And he loves Christmas.
He adores the snow you know.
Once he tried to make an angel out of pizza dough.
He's always out finding us mistletoe.
One minute he's edging up the hill,
The next he's sledging down again,
"Weeeee!"
Sometimes he even climbs the tree,
When he hears the bells,
He yells so loud,
I'm telling you he could shift a cloud!
When it's over,
He calls himself Rover.
It would never be Christmas
Without my cat, Smifftmas!

Alanah Morris (9)

It's Christmas!

We all want to see Santa on Christmas Eve,
Rudolf the reindeer loves to fly higher and faster in the sky,
It just all makes us want to say, "Hi."
So down the chimney Santa goes,
When he is at the bottom the whole place glows.
Stacking the presents under the tree,
Having his mince pie
And his glass of whisky,
It makes him happy and full of glee.
Hurry Santa, get back up the chimney
Because here come the children
Waiting to see if there are any presents under the tree.
They love Christmas games
And forever happy they will be!

Logan Finn Stretton (13)

Winter Mornings

I wake up to find
We've had a visit from Jack Frost,
I step outside in my dressing gown,
My feet start to hurt on the cold ground,
I can see my breath drifting away.

Snowy mornings are my favourite,
Throwing snowballs and making snowmen,
Lying down and creating snow angels,
Shaking the snow off of the tree,
Snowflakes melting on my arm.

I can hear robins in the distance,
Rabbits burrow in the snow,
Dogs chasing snowflakes,
Reindeer getting ready to help Santa,
A smile on everyone's face.

Lilly Wardle (9)

A Tale Of The Wintry Forest

It's winter here,
I'm standing all alone,
Cold and dishevelled,
Hearing only the sounds of a distant moan.

There's nothing to do here,
Everything to dread,
Oh how I wish I was a bear,
So I could hibernate deep below the forest bed.

Standing tall,
Observing the pale, wintry sky,
Before I turn away,
I see the stunning robins gracefully fly by.

As night draws closer,
I long for my canopy,
And you may start to question, what am I?
But now you may know,
I am a tree.

Kea Wyles (10)

Winter Dreams

Looked out of my window.
"It's Christmas!" I called.
When little white snowflakes started to fall
I sprinted downstairs with glee,
But nearly knocked over the Christmas tree!

I put on my warm clothes and ran outside,
Cold it was,
Rolling snow for a snowman,
Whilst singing about Santa Claus!

I built my snowman, it stood with pride,
Though I couldn't move my jaws from side to side.
Time for roast dinner, with cranberry sauce,
The best thing about Christmas is eating of course!

Mollie Wragg (11)

Winter Days

You deliver the 'boo' to other neighbours
Added to any spooky favours
Fireworks whizzing down and around
Gazing at the terrific hissing all over town
The sky has turned to witching hour and the Earth is frozen
The world is relaxing on this wintry night.

We are a fun group, we like to share the fun
So please help us to keep the 'boo' and save the stun
From the fire, there is a vile smell
Of all the smoke you could probably tell
The stars are bright
I spread my arms and take flight...

Isabella India Scull (11)

White Flake Of Snow

A little patterned flake of snow
Floated effortlessly through the crisp cold sky.

It sparkled in the moonlight,
Its beaming essence glows
Like one light in a sea of dark.

It drifted down onto the grass
And lay on the ground lifeless.

The wind lightly blew and the snowflake lifted up.
Moving again slowly and steady,
Flying past the children laughing and playing inside.

Sparkles fell as it travelled over the town, waving,
As the snowflake flew off into the night.

Olivia Kellier (13)

Christmas Is Here

As Christmas starts to arrive
Everyone is starting to get excited
For Santa and his elves
For giving and receiving
And it's starting to snow
Snow is exciting
But the cold that will come is biting
As we dream of the sun
It still snows
Let it snow, let it snow!

S anta riding on his sleigh
A s the reindeer pull Santa across the sky
N early at their destination
T heir presents quite heavy
A nd they're finally at their destination.

Erin Kenzie (9)

Wintertime

The wind lifted me up into the breeze
Where I sang in the rhythm of the snow that fell
Swaying in the tune of the Northern Lights
Frozen in timeless melody.

The stars will show us the way to go
While the singers in the snow will bring us the joy
You can make a big snowman and put a carrot as his nose
But sadly I am too short to do so.

Snow is falling all around
The trees are up and presents are there
The time has come where we join as one
Christmas time has finally come.

Valishia Bhakta (10)

Snowflakes, Snowflakes

Snowflakes, snowflakes
I love it when it snows
I love to make snowballs and throw them

Snowflakes, snowflakes
I love to make a snowman
Make it fat and make its carrot nose

Snowflakes, snowflakes
How delightful, how pleasant
Christmas is here, it's bright and cold

Snowflakes, snowflakes
Frightful outside, delightful inside
Snowflakes, snowflakes
Hot chocolate will be a delight
Marshmallow will be exciting
Snowflakes, snowflakes, snowflakes.

Gianna Efanam Tsikata (7)

Wintertime

W arm and cosy fires
 I love sledging in the white, crisp snow
N aughty snowballs going everywhere
 T ime to eat lots of chocolate every night
 E very animal starts to hibernate
 R eading curled up on the comfy sofa
 T ime to do snow angels and build snow forts
 I love cold, crisp winters with snow falling
M mm, marshmallows in hot chocolate on a cold day
 E veryone plays in the soft snow happily.

I love winter!

Hannah Lucy Smith (8)

Merry Christmas!

Christmas is here,
It's time to celebrate.
Families and friends gather together
For a nice roast meal.
We play and open presents!

Everybody is happy
On Christmas Eve.
Christmas is here,
It's time to celebrate.
We play and have snowball fights
In the cold, icy and and shivering snow.

Christmas Eve is a fun
And enjoyable festival to celebrate.
I give you this poem
To say merry Christmas to everyone!
Merry Christmas everybody!

Adyan Najm (9)

The Snow Scenery

The stars all winking at you,
As the snow falls from the sky.
Children scream with delight,
All eager to go outside and play,
But the children are wrapped
Around the warmth of their home.

S ee icicles hanging from trees.
N ever-ending snow falling from the sky.
O h people cry as snow starts to melt!
W inter is nearly gone.

It's time to say bye-bye!
It's time for me to go,
I got, a snow scenery to catch, yo!

Jahanavee Sandeep (9)

Christmas

Christmas, Christmas all around,
Christmas snow lies on the ground.
Baubles decorate each tree,
Tinsel wreaths surround you and me.

Carol singers sing all night,
Christmas lights, a lovely sight.
Santa Claus' sleigh bells ring,
And hear the church bells *ding, dong, ding.*

Angels light up all the skies,
As Jesus in his manger lies.
Shepherd and wise men present him with gifts,
But Mary in her arms does lift.

Dana Clare Dagostino (11)

The Meaning Of Christmas?

As the snow danced its way to the ground
The deer hooves will pound and pound.
The memory of that distinct sound
Is what makes Christmas so profound.

The kids are laughing
While they are sleighing.
Presents are opening.
Gifts are sharing.

But is this all Christmas is about
Or has it got a bigger amount
Of meaning,
Of love
That we should cherish
Or will the real meaning
Of Christmas simply perish?

Emmeline Sara Harkins (12)

Winter Is The Best

A silent night, a star above
A blessed gift of love
Outside it's bitter cold
Yet there're Christmas presents to be sold.
Winter is here!
Families sitting around the crackling fire.
Listening to the Christmas choir.

Santa is here
Dad's opening beers
Winter is here
Inside, children sipping hot cocoa
Sniffling at the sweet aroma of mince pies
Winter is the best!

Tia Miah (15)

Seasonal Sensations

The leaves are falling,
Yellow, red and brown,
All the different colours falling all around.
As the season, autumn slowly goes away,
The season, winter is heading our way.
Snow is falling from the sky to the ground,
Snowmen with carrot noses,
Snowflakes and children with little red button noses.
As spring arrives there is no snow
Cos winter says it's time to go.

Catriona Erin Steele (9)

Hot Chocolate

H appily sipping away,
O n a beautiful painted table,
T he best drink ever,

C ocoa explosion,
H eat rising from the cup,
O h, so amazing,
C reamy hot milk,
O h, so delicious,
L ovely and warm,
A lways having marshmallows,
T errific taste,
E xtraordinary flavours!

Milly Miles-Shenton (9)

Winter

Winter is here
Christmas is near
Dark, cold days
With snow on its way
With Christmas lights on
And carols outside
It's freezing cold but really nice
I love the snow
It's snowmen that stand
In a snowy, white land
I love the snow
White and clean
The snow falls down to my feet
Winter is here
Christmas is near.

Leah Miah (12)

Let It Snow

Let it snow,
Let winter come,
Let happiness flow
And let the holidays begin.

Let winter enchant you,
With its beauty everywhere.
Winter is amazing,
Just like the other seasons.
Winter is here.

Happiness is everywhere,
With every step you take,
Happiness is there.

Let it snow with happiness.

Nursel Albayrak (10)

In Winter

In winter it's cold and makes you freeze
And it makes you sneeze
In winter it's foggy
And I even saw a doggy
In winter I went to church
And I was wearing a warm shirt

In winter I listened to the beat
And it was cold on the street
In winter there was a dog
And it was chasing a green frog
In winter my sister was wearing mittens
And I wish I had kittens!

Zack Kiraga (6)

Let It Snow!

Let it snow!
Let it snow!
No need to say I know.
It is fun when it snows,
When it snows there's a happy glow.
Let it snow!
Let it snow!
We need a happy glow,
People will have snowball fights
And enjoy the beautiful sight,
You could wear gloves so the frost doesn't bite.
Let it snow!
Let it snow!

Abdulaahi Abukar (9)

Christmas Is Going

Winter is here,
Summer is over.
It's time to celebrate,
I'm another year older.

The snow is so deep,
I will build a snowman.
It's time to go in,
To eat Christmas dinner.

The snow is all gone,
Melted into the river.
I loved Christmas Day,
And a happy New Year.

Chloe Elizabeth Padgett (12)

The Winter Snow

Snow, snow,
I can hear Santa saying, "Ho, ho, ho!"
Waiting for Santa all night,
I can't wait to see his height.
With Rudolph with his bright nose
And Santa with his frozen toes.
Snowflakes are falling,
I can hear Father Christmas calling.

Olivia Rose Hayes (10)

Winter

W ondering when he might come.

I cicles hanging.

N apkins set on our festive table.

T ime to wrap Christmas presents.

E veryone together at the table.

R ed robin has come to keep an eye on me.

Mia Nicholls (9)

Little Jesus Is Born

Little Jesus is born
He is as little as corn
In a stable
Which rhymes with table
Lays in a manger
But he is not a stranger
And angels sing
"Glory to the newborn king..."
The next day they are smiling
When they see him sparkling.

Weronika Lubinska (10)

Winter

W arming hot chocolate
 I n my lap.
N ot a single cookie left
T hat I haven't eaten.
E very day I try to
R emember to leave cookies and milk for Santa.

Rojin Kaya (10)

All Things Snow

S nowflakes, snowmen, all around.
N ight sky, floodlight for the town.
O nly melts when it's warm summertime.
W inter wonderland, time to shine.

Riya Kaur (9)

The Winter Night

The snow was as white as a cloud.
The snow was as fluffy as a dog's fur.
The snow was as cold as ice.
The sky was as dark as a black hole.

Chloe Nixon (6)

Polar Bears

Oh! The snowy polar bears,
I wish, I wish, I wish
I could be there with you!

Blair Stewart (5)

A Snowy Day

Kids are playing in the snow.
Mums and dads are taking their children to a show.
With Father Christmas along the way,
He says, "Ho, ho, ho!"
And after that I hear a little knock on the door.
"Ho, ho, ho!" It's Father Christmas at the door,
He gives us presents on Christmas Day.
I go to bed and I go to sleep.

Alexandra Sachinis (6)
Blackheath High School, Blackheath

Snowflakes

Snowflakes, oh snowflakes,
All of them around,
They only come at Christmas,
And only if you're around.
Only if you have a soft, gentle hand.
You will only get pneumonia
If you don't wrap up warm
And when you get home,
A nice fire will be lit
Then you will sit in bed
All nice and warm.

Sofia Ashley-Jones (8)
Blackheath High School, Blackheath

Christmas

Everyone's been waiting, excited, overjoyed,
Only the turkey is really annoyed.
Christmas tree up, angel on top,
Cards, decorations, oh the lot!
Candy canes, chocolate and sweets,
Sell in every shop you meet.
Carols are sung,
Christmas has begun,
And then, Santa comes.

Maria Godina (9)
Blackheath High School, Blackheath

Untitled

There's a chill and the snowflakes flow,
They're really delicate.
Snowflakes float,
Perhaps waiting for snow to go ice skating,
Sledging or huddling in front of the fire,
Drinking chocolate milk.
When it's winter
You get a splinter
And also especially Kinder.

Darcey O'Toole-Dincov (7)
Blackheath High School, Blackheath

Snowflakes

Snowflakes fall from the mysterious sky
Into the freezing white snow.
They fly in the breeze onto my tongue.
Snowflakes make winter cool and cheerful.
Snowflakes are delicate.
They melt on your tongue, making a cool drink.
I love snowflakes.

Emma Harris (9)
Blackheath High School, Blackheath

It Is Snowing, It Is Snowing

It is snowing, it is snowing
Let all the robins sing
It is snowing, it is snowing
The trees are covered with snow
It is snowing, it is snowing
Everybody is singing
Everybody is dancing
Because it is Christmas Day.

Beatrice Montgomery (6)
Blackheath High School, Blackheath

Winter

Hot chocolate in front of a fireplace,
Trees jingling, full of balls,
Frosted windows,
And pearly-white snow falls.
Reindeer and sleighs fly in my dream,
When I'm warm and tucked up in bed.
I like winter.

Angelina Yingna Wu (10)
Blackheath High School, Blackheath

Snow

S now crystals falling gently from the sky
N ice warm fires to block out the falling snow's cold
O pen doors with singing and warmth
W inter is here, the best time of all the year.

Emily Soulsby (9)
Blackheath High School, Blackheath

Snowy Days

Snowflakes falling
Snowballs are cold
Nobody could have dreamed of this weather
Kids are playing in the snow
And building a snowman
And throwing snowballs.

Ela Kaya (6)
Blackheath High School, Blackheath

Snowing Down

Snowing down,
Snowing down,
Kids are playing in the cold,
Not a sound,
Not a sound,
Snowing down.

Emily Hancock (7)
Blackheath High School, Blackheath

One Snowy Day

One snowy day
I touched the glass on the window
It was freezing
And I went outside to play.

Lucy Godina (7)
Blackheath High School, Blackheath

Untitled

Winter is fun
Winter is fun
Because you can make a snowman
And snow angels.

Meiling Chu (6)
Blackheath High School, Blackheath

I Love Christmas

I love to ski at Christmas
It makes me happy
I wear warm clothes when I ski.

Eva Violet Chirmiciu (5)
Blackheath High School, Blackheath

68

Untitled

As the sun fell and the night woke up,
The snow began to drop dead.
As the fantasies of young children's dream day burn up
I lay motionless as I ponder about the legend
Of an old man breaking in to give me a gift.

He would stumble and fall,
While the millennials laugh in your face.
They severely lack respect or grace.
I still ponder and frolic with my mind.

Why leave milk and cookies out
For someone who isn't there?
Why go through the pain
Of carol singers knocking on your door
When you could ignore them?

Why?
I'll tell you why,
Because society wants to frustrate you
And possibly give meaning to life itself
And it's kind of sad.

Happy holidays.

Jennifer Morgan (12)
Buckler's Mead Academy, Yeovil

Winter Is Coming

Leaves are falling off the huge, bulky trees,
You won't see anymore black and yellow bees.
The beautiful hot summer is in the past,
The freezing cold winter is here at last.

It's time to get out a warm scarf and hat,
And maybe even dress up your cold, little cat.
You might want to buy a warm fleece coat,
To make sure you don't get an awful sore throat.

It's nearly time to put up that big Christmas tree,
And look out the window to see kids shining with glee.
Decorate the tree with lots of bits and bobs,
Make sure to put your delicious hot food on the hobs.

Get your warm blankets at the ready,
Because that cold winter weather doesn't look too steady.
Turn your heating up to stay nice and cosy,
Just enough to keep your cheeks red and rosy.

It's time to get excited, snowflakes are falling,
Make sure you get up early in the morning.
When Santa arrives, be on look-out,
Soon he will be going back up the chimney spout.

When you wake up and get out of your bed,
You look out the window and see snow on the shed.
Look under the tree, there's lots of presents,
Oh my god, it's a new pet pheasant!

Alisha Wilde (12)

Buckler's Mead Academy, Yeovil

Christmas!

C arol singers by the fire, the children are starting to get a little bit tired.

H umbug is something you never want to hear, instead you should spread the Christmas cheer.

R epeat the songs and sing along while the church bells go *ding-dong*.

I love making the decorations and putting them up but putting the star on really gives that finishing touch.

S anta's coming! Quick let's get going!

T imer's beeping, roast is done, now it's turkey for you, me and everyone.

M any sad times have passed now, hopefully joy will join us at last.

A ll the presents under the tree, Santa left them just for me.

S tockings all hung on the door, who could ask for anything more?

Keira Stevenson (12)
Buckler's Mead Academy, Yeovil

Animals In Winter

A nimals are beautiful things that live and grow
N ever scared of anything, they play with snow
I gloos are where the polar bears go
M issing out on all the fun
A re the polar bears
L eaving where they live because of the snow?
S obbing are the children who want to go home

I nhabited with nowhere to go
N ever seeing their parents again

W illing to do anything to see them again
I gloos keep them safe and warm
N ot wanting to stay inside
T hey run away to find somewhere to hide
E ven though it starts to snow
R eally they just want to be happy again.

Keegan Bond (12)
Buckler's Mead Academy, Yeovil

A Snow Day

As winter falls,
So does night,
Earlier and earlier,
It's no longer bright.

I stir my hot cocoa,
It's all nice and warm,
It's topped with whipped cream
And marshmallows too.

In the day I play in the snow,
Wearing my scarf and gloves,
I wish we could get snowed in,
Sitting by the fire all day.

As I come in for dinner,
It's all cosy and warm,
I have a hot water bottle in bed,
I wish I could do it all again.

Cody Isaacs (12)
Buckler's Mead Academy, Yeovil

Winter Snow

W inter is coming very soon,
 I t is time for a new winter tune,
 N ever forget those happy times,
 T hat moment the Christmas bells chime,
 E ven though we've had our fun,
 R emember this year, a new one has begun.

 S now is cold just like me,
 N ow I am sat under a tree,
 O n the ice river where children play,
 W inter will stay for one more day.

Jamie-Leigh Rose (11)
Buckler's Mead Academy, Yeovil

You Know It's Winter

You know it's winter,
When you hear Christmas songs.

You know it's winter,
When the frosty breeze makes you shiver.

You know it's winter,
When you hear sleigh bells ringing.

You know it's winter,
When snow falls delicately.

You know it's winter,
When Christmas lights are on.

You know it's winter,
When Christmas is coming.

Hannah Beedle (13)
Buckler's Mead Academy, Yeovil

Christmas Eve

The sparkle from the Christmas tree,
Glistens right in front of me,
Winter is here,
Frost all around,
Christmas is near,
Snow is the ground.

Hot chocolate in my hand,
Playing in the winter sand,
Snow in my hair,
Christmas spirit everywhere.

Christmas Eve I lie in bed,
Excited for the day ahead,
Presents wrapped under the tree,
Lots of them are just for me.

Carrie Jackson (12)
Buckler's Mead Academy, Yeovil

Rudolph

R iding through the snow we go.

U nder and over Santa's sleigh goes!

D ancer and Prancer are Rudolph's best friends.

O nly happiness this Christmas!

L aughter as the children hear, "Ho, ho, ho."

P eople wonder where he rides off to in the sky.

H a, you'll never know where Santa's sleigh goes.

Ellie-Mai Lauchlan (11)
Buckler's Mead Academy, Yeovil

Christmas Night

As hedgehogs crawl under logs,
The church bells chime,
While families drink lemon and lime
And the little birds cheep,
While the children sleep,
The horses neigh,
As Santa goes past on his sleigh,
The reindeer's nose is glowing,
While white circles are snowing,
It is Christmas night!

Jessica Pitman (12)
Buckler's Mead Academy, Yeovil

A Winter Day

Winter is a magnificent time of year,
Listen, listen to the birds singing on the icicle lake,
Listen, listen to the carol singers at the church,
Listen, listen to the bells ringing at midnight
And listen to the people cheering because it's Christmas.

Ellie Kirkpatrick (13)
Buckler's Mead Academy, Yeovil

Winter

W arm inside by the open fire
I cy ponds
N ight-time dark and cold
T emperature decreases to minus
E xcited for Christmas
R udolph running through the snow.

Christian Hobson (12)
Buckler's Mead Academy, Yeovil

Winter Is Here!

In the dark night
When I've shut my eyes
A breeze comes through the window, awakening me.
I get up and take my dressing gown,
I take a look outside of my window...
Winter is here.

Madison Dummer (12)
Buckler's Mead Academy, Yeovil

The Perfect Christmas

What we all love about Christmas Eve
Is that it is the day before Christmas
Little children leaving food out for Santa and Rudolph
Hoping that Santa will leave something in return.

Everyone together watching a movie at night
Outside there is no one in sight
Children go to bed early so Santa can come
They hope to hear his sleigh bells ring.

In the morning it is Christmas Day
And it is filled with madness all the way
With opening presents, being filled with cheer
To pulling crackers and cooking Christmas dinners.

We look out the window to see the snow fall
The pile of snow starts to grow tall
Everyone is filled with cheer
To spend time with ones near.

Children start their thank you letters to Santa
While drinking a hot cup of cocoa
Everyone is then sad to hear
That Christmas is over for another year.

April McGookin (13)
Carrickfergus College, Carrickfergus

Christmas Spirit

Our wreath is finally on the door,
Presents scattered all over the floor.
Waiting eagerly for Santa to come,
Knowing that Christmas has only just begun.

It's now December, it's cold and dark,
Our days are over in the park.
Hats, scarves and gloves are needed,
Every day this is repeated.

Kids are playing in the snow,
But soon they will have to go.
They build snowmen and have snowball fights,
While their mother turns on the Christmas lights.

As we arrive home from school,
There is a chill, the air is cool.
We sit down at the fireplace,
We rush upstairs as it is a race.

We lie down on our beds,
We then rest our heads.
It's morning, we are another day closer,
My sister is taking Christmas pictures,
She is such a poser!

I can't believe,
OMG! It's Christmas Eve.
We rush around preparing for tomorrow,
I just go with the flow and hope for snow.

I hear a bang and a crash,
I hope Santa doesn't get covered in ash.
I debate with myself whether to wake up,
I just hope I get a pup.

It's finally here, it's Christmas Day,
Last time I checked it was a month away.
Unfortunately I didn't get a puppy,
But the greatest gift I already have is my family.

Though Christmas is not just about gifts,
As you know it's not a myth,
This holiday is to celebrate Jesus' birth,
And you should already know what it's worth.

It is over, Christmas is gone,
No more snow on our lawn.
There is no more Christmas cheer,
Guess we will have to wait again till next year.

Kate Neill (14)
Carrickfergus College, Carrickfergus

Untitled

It's twelve days before Christmas
And at night, the Christmas lights are glowing
This makes me feel happy and excited
That's why it's my favourite time of year.

Santa and his elves are working around the clock
To make sure every day boys and girls
Get the toys that they have asked for,
Remember only the ones whose names are on the nice list
Will receive their presents from Santa
As naughty children only get left a sack of coal.

It's Christmas Eve and I'm tucked up in bed
I couldn't get to sleep because I was so excited
To know what Santa has left for me
As I've tried my best to be good all year
It's 3am and I tiptoe down the stairs
To peek at what he has left for me
When suddenly the living room door opens
And a man in a red suit appears
I stand there in shock
My feet stuck to the floor
His hand reached out to touch me
I quickly closed my eyes
Then felt a gentle tap on my shoulder
And when I opened my eyes

To my amazement it was my mum
Standing over me in bed
Telling me Santa has been
I felt I already knew this
But it must have been a dream.

Niamh Alexander (13)
Carrickfergus College, Carrickfergus

The Boy Who Saved (His) Christmas

I can't wait till Christmas
It's only tomorrow
Then I can open presents
And eat Christmas dinner.

It's finally here
It's Christmas Day
I run downstairs
Only to see there's nothing under the tree.

Then I hear a crash, bang and clatter
Someone's in my house
He must have stolen my presents
I must chase him down.

I run after him, out the back door
He's trying to climb the fence
I mustn't let him get away
What has become of Christmas Day?

I pick up a football and kick it
It hits him on the head
He falls back down and can't get back up
Because I'm sitting on him till the police come.

My adrenaline's running
At least I saved Christmas
For me anyway.

Matthew Ashe (13)
Carrickfergus College, Carrickfergus

My Type Of Christmas

My type of Christmas is...
shopping for gifts for the people I love.
My type of Christmas is...
eating lots of chocolatey Christmas sweets.
My type of Christmas is...
cosying up by the fire with a sweet, hot drink.
My type of Christmas is...
eating a big turkey dinner surrounded by family.
My type of Christmas is...
decorating the tree and lighting up my house.
My type of Christmas is...
coming downstairs and seeing all the presents
ready to be opened.
My type of Christmas is...
spending time together and having a good time!

Casey Holmes (14)
Carrickfergus College, Carrickfergus

Two Christmases, One Christmas

Opening presents on Christmas Day
It is such a joy
But outside there some children sleep
They don't even get one toy.

For some it's about cookies and milk
The dinner on the table
But for others it is difficult to bring
The ones who are not able.

We tend to overlook these things
Most are not like them
But Christmas is a time for caring
Even if not 'a gem'.

No two Christmases are alike
We know that is for sure
But both should have the same meaning
No matter, rich or poor.

Joshua Miller (14)
Carrickfergus College, Carrickfergus

Walking Around

We are picking a Christmas tree
We have lowered it down to three
We are picking a Christmas tree
We have to take a break.

We are in a cafe
Mum having a latte
Dad complaining about weight
And I'm having a light milkshake.

Going back
We pick a tree and it starts snowing
It has been packed
I am going home now.

Merry Christmas everyone
Christmas is here
Merry Christmas everyone
And a happy New Year.

Oliver Boyce (14)
Carrickfergus College, Carrickfergus

Christmas

We've put up the Christmas tree,
Sitting beside it is where I want to be,
There are thousands of presents under it,
You'll get one surely if you've been a good kid.

When I see the Christmas tree,
It always fills me up with glee,
The Christmas tree and all the snow,
Soon we'll have to let them go.

Tony Yordanov (14)
Carrickfergus College, Carrickfergus

Let It Snow

Christmas is coming
Winter is here
But you shouldn't fear, if you've been good all year
You can finally be free under the Christmas tree
Cackling and laughing away
Christmas is coming;
Christmas is near
Winter is here
The big fat man is coming.

Stephen Gould (14)
Carrickfergus College, Carrickfergus

Let It Snow

It starts to snow
Children are getting excited
Santa is coming soon
As our decorations are going up
The air gets colder by the day
Until the day, 24th December
Everyone, excited for one reason
Santa is coming tonight...

Aaron McCalmont (14)
Carrickfergus College, Carrickfergus

This One Of A Kind Winter's Night

Brrr! What's that I see?
People already starting to freeze.
The frosty breeze dancing in the air,
As families are coming to share,
On this one of a kind winter's night.
Christmas cheer spreading through the night
To children near and far
On this one of a kind winter's night.
The clock strikes midnight
And paper starts to tear,
Gifts revealed everywhere,
It's like everyone's wishes just came true,
Not just for me but you guys too,
On this one of a kind winter's night.
Children all over the world
Are squealing with cheer...
Merry Christmas, Noel
And Feliz Navidad!
While Santa hides behind a blanket of stars,
On this one of a kind winter's night.

Yaana Seewoolall (12)

Harris Academy, Morden

Winter

Finally, winter is here,
Let's all gather around the Christmas tree and cheer!

You can smell the cinnamon and the pine needles,
As by the fire the adults are sharing riddles.

We are brave and bold,
So we put on some warm winter clothes,
Everyone is ready to face the merciless cold,
Thick woollen socks to protect everyone's toes.

The children are riding their sleighs,
Down the hills blanketed with their snow,
They're having fun in so many ways,
Back home, they no longer want to go.

At dusk, the streets and pavements go mute,
All you can hear are the owls that hoot.

The snow on the ground feels so warm and deep,
Over delicate flowers that lie asleep.

Ida Paradowska (13)
Harris Academy, Morden

Snowflakes

No snowflake is the same or identical,
No snowflake is weird
But always wonderful.
Snowflakes are special,
Wonderful, magical things,
Just like friendship.
No friendship is the same or identical,
No friendship is weird
But always wonderful.
Friendships are special,
A magical thing.
Friendship takes layers,
Like the layers of snow outside,
This is why friendship blooms.
Once you have it you will always know
That you will never be alone.
Merry Christmas.

Voichita Bura
Harris Academy, Morden

Christmas

The snow is falling
The fire is roaring
It's Christmas Eve, the countdown has begun
The carollers have been round and sung
Brushing my teeth, getting ready for bed
Hoping to catch a glimpse of the man in red
The milk has been poured and carrots laid out
Hoping I've made the good list
I've already eaten my sprouts.

Christmas morning, I'm awake at four!
Thanks to my excited little brother knocking on my door
We head down the stairs to see if the food has gone
There was nothing there, he'd even nicked a scone!
I went into the living room to look under the tree
And to my surprise there was a PS3!

Thomas Prewett (11)
King James' School, Almondbury

The True Meaning Of Christmas

Christmas is a time for laughter,
Not just because of the coming of Santa,
It's watching and skating on ice,
It's the natural things that make it great,
Like watching the squirrels hibernate,

Or sending Christmas cards to your loved one,
And eyeing at the short days that come,
For Christians, the birth of Jesus is key,

Christmas carols in the air,
A time for all of us to share,
This warm and fuzzy feeling,
Youngsters excited, shouting and squealing,

As they see the first snowflake falling,
It will never get boring!
Nobody can really catch the meaning of Christmas,
Because it is so much more than the kisses,
The presents that we get,
The latest Xbox 2X,
There are no words to describe the beautiful time we all see,
The starry night, the glistening trees,

It's a shame the Grinch didn't see it too,
Because for the rest of his life he remained blue,
To all I just want to say,
Merry Christmas and enjoy your day!

Beata Anna Palasz (11)

King James' School, Almondbury

Santa's Arrived!

As I looked into the sky,
I saw a sparkle flying high,
As I stared I saw a glisten,
That's when I began to listen.

A shadow filled the sky,
It quickly caught my eye,
I blinked and it disappeared
And the sky was plain and dark.

My heart skipped a beat,
As I jumped up onto my feet,
I heard a thud on the roof,
Followed by the clattering of a hoof.

I scrambled up the stairs,
Like an excited bear,
Then I opened up the window
And looked out in awe,
Santa had arrived on his sleigh,
I was so excited. Hip hip hooray!

Amelia Kate Chaplin
King James' School, Almondbury

This Christmas Morning

Presents scattered all around,
Snow is falling to the ground,
Children will soon make a sound
On this Christmas morning.

Gingerbread and Christmas trees,
Santa and his magic keys,
An icy wind, a wintry breeze
On this Christmas morning.

Stars are shining, big and bright,
Twinkling like a Christmas light,
Reindeer soar on their long flight
On this Christmas morning.

Christmas jumpers, festive treats,
Over-indulging on sweets,
Around the table, lots of seats,
Merry Christmas morning.

Brook Seed (11)
King James' School, Almondbury

Christmas Morning

'Twas Christmas morning,
All the parents, yawning,
As the children cried with glee.

All the family gathered,
As the surprises were revealed,
Then the party began.

The family danced,
As it was finally announced,
And everyone jumped with joy.

They danced all day,
They sang all night,
Until it was the very next morning.

Beckie Hodge (11)
King James' School, Almondbury

The Gift Of Giving

Snowflakes on noses,
Cover dead leaves and roses,
Kids at the park having fun.
Snowmen in gardens,
Homes dressed with garlands,
These are the happy days for some.
A fun-loving family,
Gifts round the tree,
Christmas is a happy time for kids like me.
Yet my thoughts turn to others,
Who have no warm covers,
No home and no gifts to receive.

Grace Throssell (12)
King James' School, Almondbury

Hibernation

Now summer's over and autumn's gone
The months of winter have begun
We get the frost, we get the snow
That's when animals go below
Below the ground to keep them warm
To keep them safe and away from harm
They sleep for months, till warmth comes around
And hopefully wake up safe and sound.

Benjamin Robert Copley (11)
King James' School, Almondbury

Winter

The snow is thick on the ground,
The trees are coated in a white blanket,
Animals settle down for the winter,
Wrapped up warm for the snow,
We sledge down the snow-capped hills,
The snow is thick on the ground,
It's winter.

Morgan John Kirk (12)
King James' School, Almondbury

The Winter

When the air is cold,
The animals are packing away,
The roads are freezing,
The water magically turns to ice
And the first snowflakes touch the floor...
The winter comes.
The children sing,
The snow comes,
The snowman comes alive
And the Christmas spirit is dancing in the air.
Santa is making presents,
You come home,
The Christmas tree says hello,
You stand around the warm fire
To wait for the next day.
You stay with your friends, relaxing,
You hear the Christmas bells,
That's the Christmas spirit
To see the good children.
You see a light, they are here!
You go ice skating or you go to ski.
You go home and you have a special dinner.
At night you hear a, "Ho, ho, ho!"
That's the Christmas sleigh
With Santa and the eight reindeer!

You wake to see if you've got presents
Calling all your family and you go to play.
Christmas is for family and fun
And a snowman is created from snow
So... let it snow!

Laura Gancia (7)
La Scuola Italiana A Londra, London

The Winter Breeze

The pale winter morning when you wake up,
A cold breeze softly brushes your face,
A sweet, quiet tune, the wind seems to bring,
As if from a magical world in a fairytale book,
The time stops and your legs fail to move,
A wondrous look carved on your face.
Not so long after the wind just moves on,
The soft and calm melody going with it.
And still at night when you are fast asleep,
You dream of that beautiful song,
The lullaby making you sleep.
Not many words can explain this song well,
Fantastic, mysterious; the list just goes on!
But to end this poem, once and for all,
We will just call it... the winter breeze.

Julia Alice Pensa (10)
La Scuola Italiana A Londra, London

Merry Christmas

M erry Christmas everyone,

E veryone is having fun with snowboards,

R *ing, ring, dong, ding,*

R *ing, ring, ding ding,*

Y eah!

C hristmas, Christmas is coming,

H ot chocolate is yummy and hot,

R eindeer are helping Santa, ho, ho, ho!

I t's fun playing with friends and making

S nowmen!

T urkey and Brussels sprouts are ready cooked to eat,

M aking decorations so Santa knows where to put the presents,

A wreath is all ready to put up on the door,

S anta, I can't wait for the 25th December.

Federica Collavo (9)
La Scuola Italiana A Londra, London

Merry Christmas

M erry Christmas everyone.
E veryone is waiting for Santa.
R ide the new snow mobile.
R eunited with family and friends.
Y eah! Holiday time is the best!

C hrist was born on this day.
H is for holy.
R eindeer are flying in the air.
I n this magic day
S ongs, dance and happy games.
T ry to think nice. Which
M agical present you will get?
A nd Santa comes with a sack.
S uper fantastic Christmas days!

Tommaso Lombardo (8)
La Scuola Italiana A Londra, London

Christmas

C ome on everyone, Santa is almost here!

"**H** o, ho, ho! I'm here on the rooftop."

R inging bells from the rooftop.

I think I might go straight to bed.

S anta is almost down the rooftop.

T aking my teddy bear and going to bed without being seen

M erry Christmas everyone!

A s soon as he left I went in the living room,

S eeing the empty plate and the empty cup. I thought Santa might have enjoyed the milk and the cookies.

Edoardo Pallotti (8)
La Scuola Italiana A Londra, London

Untitled

As the frost bites,
You can hear a tingling song.
Endless melodies,
Coming from the sky above.
Nature freezes to hear his song,
As it draws you in and there's no escape.
When it finally passes,
Nature and others are sleeping,
As plants wither up and die.
No one knows what this song is or does
But that is what I can do,
To explain this to you
As I have lived this experience,
A truly wonderful one it was,
For winter is the season it used to be.

Caterina Annabelle Berg (9)
La Scuola Italiana A Londra, London

Christmas Tree

Christmas tree, big and bright
Christmas tree, shining and decorated
Next to the fire,
Here you leave some food for Father Christmas
When Father Christmas comes
He eats the food then he leaves some presents
Under the Christmas tree.
When the decorations and stars shine
Then he flies away with his reindeer
And even the reindeer eat the food.
Then when you wake up, you open the presents.
When Christmas is over you put away the Christmas tree.

Eleonora Terranova (6)
La Scuola Italiana A Londra, London

Merry Christmas

M y best Christmas ever,
E ven of the weather,
R eindeer come here,
R udolph will come near,
Y eah it's Christmas!

C ome on, it's Christmas,
H ear the noise,
R ead to Santa Claus,
I s Christmas everywhere,
S anta, give me presents!
T he best comes from Santa,
M y new toys,
A game for boys,
S anta, Santa, thank you!

Michele Pediconi (8)
La Scuola Italiana A Londra, London

Christmas Eve

Sitting by the fireplace
A letter to Santa tied in a green lace
The tree has nothing underneath
And I help my brother put up the wreath
My sister is cuddled on the sofa in a shiny, pink sheet
And is swelling down to her feet
The picture of a rose
And Rudolph's bright red nose.
Christmas can be magic
But because of Jesus' death it can be tragic
So I'm happy to know
You will play in the snow!

Camilla Moni (9)
La Scuola Italiana A Londra, London

Christmas Is Coming

Christmas is coming,
Better get running,
Christmas carols,
Yummy puddings,
Santa on his way,
Taking off with his sleigh,
Reindeer having their last bite of carrot.
To every country in the world,
They soar though the night sky,
Bringing you presents!
But don't get nosey in the night
For you're going to be good this year.
If you don't...
You are not going to have presents!

Clotilde Paino (7)
La Scuola Italiana A Londra, London

It's Christmas!

The children will open their presents.
It's time to build a snowman
And play with the snow.
Remake the new Christmas tree.
When everyone is happy, Christmas comes.

It's so exciting to be delighted at Christmas!
At Christmas you get loved.
At Christmas it is fun!
At Christmas Santa comes.
At Christmas presents come.
It is lovely to have a family in a house,
With a mouse!

Aurora Pandolfi (8)
La Scuola Italiana A Londra, London

Christmas

S anta will come very soon
A mazing presents will come to you
N on-stop laughing
T hank Santa a lot
A dventurous Christmas

C ome on, open the presents
L isten to the bells
A nxiously waiting for Santa
U nbelievable dinner as well
S uper family and friends and even my dog is celebrating.

Merry Christmas!

Samuele Lombardo (11)
La Scuola Italiana A Londra, London

Christmas Crystals

Bells are ringing,
Kids are singing,
Christmas is coming,
Santa is stunning.

Children are waiting for presents to be given,
Reindeer are waiting to be driven,
Hot chocolate arriving,
Come on Christmas, we are starving!

Presents are packed,
Waiting to be unwrapped,
Tables are packed with every dish,
Waiting for the children to make a wish.

Sofia Visona (8)
La Scuola Italiana A Londra, London

Untitled

Christmas is coming, presents are coming,
Ring, ring, ding, dong, Merry Christmas everyone.
Building the Christmas tree on Christmas Eve,
Hot chocolate is prepared
But remember to eat turkey and bread.
Open the presents and see what is in them.
Balls and jerseys for boys,
Toys and clothes for girls.
Merry Christmas everyone!

Tommaso Sartore (9)
La Scuola Italiana A Londra, London

Untitled

Christmas is coming
People rejoicing
Scrumptious meals are waiting to be gobbled up.

Families join together
Having fun, chatting
Father Christmas comes!

Presents arrive under the colourful Christmas tree
Hot chocolate is prepared
Children have fun unpacking the presents

Merry Christmas everyone!

Emma Terranova (8)
La Scuola Italiana A Londra, London

Untitled

Christmas is like a dream
It's a colourful beam
Carols to be sung
Bells to be rung

Turkey is eaten
Easter is beaten
Presents are made
None are saved

Chill in the air
Trees are bare
Cake is cut
For even the rat
A small air going round the city
Happiness!

Elena Chionsini (9) & Carlo
La Scuola Italiana A Londra, London

Untitled

Snowflakes in the air,
There is nothing beyond compare,
Christmas time is magic,
Fantastic!
Presents for me,
I open them with glee,
Christmas trees everywhere,
Wow! Very Christmassy!
Enjoy Christmas Day,
It's quite a fantastic display,
Don't forget to play,
Have a lovely day.

Henry Jackson-Proes (9)
La Scuola Italiana A Londra, London

Merry Christmas

M istletoe
E verybody together
R eindeer
R udolph
Y ear

C arol singing
H ot chocolate
R ehearsal
I cy
S nowman
T insel
M onth of December
A ngel
S now.

Vittoria Ginevra Vendramin Giardina (7)
La Scuola Italiana A Londra, London

Santa Claus

Santa Claus comes on Christmas Eve.
He brings you presents to make you happy,
Like an Xbox I asked for or anything else
That you could think of!
He drinks the milk you put out for him.
He is going to eat your cookies.
Sometimes he brings all the things you want!

William Ian Berg (6)
La Scuola Italiana A Londra, London

I Like The Snow

Last year I skated with a penguin
Because I was not able to skate.
This year I learned how to skate
With Mum and Dad.
My sister and I like seeing Santa.
He might give us some presents for Christmas.
I like the snow
Because we can play with the snow.

Virginia Elisabetta Vendramin Giardina (5)
La Scuola Italiana A Londra, London

Snowman And Winter

S now
N ovember
O ctober
W inter
M istletoe
A pple
N atural

W ind
I ce
N ativity play
T ough
E nter snow
R eindeer.

Massimo Buccollato (6)
La Scuola Italiana A Londra, London

Santa

Snowboarding and skiing in the cold snow.
A group of carol singers singing carol songs.
Nice hot chocolate in your hand, warming you up.
Turkeys and Christmas pudding gobbled up on your table.
A load of presents under your Christmas tree!

Joss Monachello (8)

La Scuola Italiana A Londra, London

Santa

S now at Christmas can be bigger and bigger
A t Christmas night, Santa comes to give presents
N ow everyone in the world is happy
T urkey is eaten by people
A t Christmas all people have presents.

Tommaso Busco (9)
La Scuola Italiana A Londra, London

Christmas

Christmas Day is here
The presents are under the tree
Now everyone is awake
And I gave Santa a cake!

The snow is falling
And everyone is playing
We are all nice and warm
We open our arms to hug.

Lucrezia Leone (10)
La Scuola Italiana A Londra, London

Christmas

Christmas is coming,
How many smiles?
Everyone is waiting for presents
And all of the children are
Watching the windows calling,
"Santa, Santa, come to me!"

Merry Christmas!

Greta Forestali (8)
La Scuola Italiana A Londra, London

Christmas

C arol singing

H ot chocolate

R eindeer

I cicles

S nowmen

T ime for family

M anger

A dvent calendar

S anta Claus.

Ettore Moni (7)
La Scuola Italiana A Londra, London

Christmas

C hocolate

H o, ho, ho!

R eindeer

I cy

S nowman

T ime for Christmas

M anger

A dvent calendars

S anta.

Giorgia Rinaldo (6)

La Scuola Italiana A Londra, London

Snow On The Ground

S now falls
N o school at all
O pen fires roar
W ondrous gifts to adore

O pening presents is fun
N oel is nearly done

T hick bows appear every year
'H ark the Herald' is sung with cheer
E xcited children all gather here

G ingerbread men are baked just in time
R inging bells jingle and chime
O rnaments hung with such great care
U nwrapping gifts hardly seems fair
N ativity scenes the country wide
D o you want to go on a sleigh ride?

Georgia Pallister (14)
Teesside High School, Eaglescliffe

When Christmas Comes Around

Christmas decorations in the town
Fires are on and family time.
Movies and snow angels
Sweets and chocolate
New pyjamas
The best time of the year has come around
No school and lots of rest
Children singing joyful carols
Santa Claus is coming soon
Children sleeping all through the night
Waiting for St Nicholas and his eight reindeer
Who bring their presents on a sleigh
They wait and listen for his last call
"Merry Christmas to all
And to all a good night!"

Mazie Mae McKenna (13)
Teesside High School, Eaglescliffe

Untitled

The excitement on Christmas morning,
Then after you have opened all your presents
It just gets boring.

An ear-splitting scream comes from my dad,
We all think it is something terribly bad.

Me and my sister run like gormless pheasants,
Into the room, I saw the enormous presents.

I saw an outline with bows all around,
The guinea pig cage is what I found.

My eyes light up for all I see,
As two little guinea pigs were staring at me.

Imogen Hall (12)
Teesside High School, Eaglescliffe

Christmas Time

Christmas time is almost here,
Santa Claus is coming near,
Fire roaring, crunching, crackling,
Outside are the carollers singing,
Lights beaming, hot chocolate steaming,
Baubles hanging on the Christmas tree,
Glimmering for everyone to see,
Stockings hung, filled to the brim,
The one who fills them, you'll never see him,
Presents wrapped, sat on the floor,
Now it's time to lock the front door,
Christmas time is here for evermore!

Ruby June Rennison (12)
Teesside High School, Eaglescliffe

Untitled

Why are there such things as a walk?
All you do is go into mud and talk.
Waste of my precious Christmas time.
There I am, just walking and whining,
While all of my friends are Christmas dining.

Then they open their gigantic gifts,
It gives everyone a joyful lift.
The experience in their houses looks cosy
Then it is the end and we see the car,
It is a horrible time going so far.

William Riley (13)
Teesside High School, Eaglescliffe

RAF Christmas

Will Dad be home for Christmas?
I really hope he is.
He flies in the sky
While I eat mince pies,
He is in the Falklands
Sending postcards of RAF planes,
I wish I was there,
To see my flight sergeant dad.

The scenery there
Is always magical,
My dad is so lucky
But I want him to come home.
Every month I wait and wait
But he never comes home.

Phoebe Croft (12)
Teesside High School, Eaglescliffe

Will I Be Home For Christmas?

Will I be home for Christmas?
Somehow I don't think so.
Snow flutters all around me,
Leaving me freezing cold.

I shiver at the memory
Of me and all my friends.
Running through lethal shooting,
Trying not to look down.

Below our feet were the fallen,
I think they're all heroes.
Giving their life to save us,
To try and stop the war.

Isabelle Blackburn (12)
Teesside High School, Eaglescliffe

For Christmas Day

Baubles shining,
Presents hiding,
Turkey is roasting,
For Christmas Day.

Fire crackling,
Outside snowing,
Chocolate melting
For Christmas Day.

Lights glowing,
Tinsel sparkling,
Biscuits crumbling
For Christmas Day.

Mum's singing,
Dad's sleeping,
Children cheering
For Christmas Day.

Emily Carney (12)
Teesside High School, Eaglescliffe

Stocking

S anta is on his way.
T he children are waiting for his sleigh.
O pening presents, it's so fun.
C ooking dinner with my mum.
K icking a football with Christmas spirit.
I n goes the ball and we win it.
N othing goes better than a family game.
G iggling at the Queen's speech of fame.

Ella Poulton (12)
Teesside High School, Eaglescliffe

Christmas

C hristmas is finally here
H undreds of presents under the tree
R unning down the stairs, so excited for presents
I was so excited for Christmas
S mell of chocolate in the air
T rees in houses full of lights
M erry Christmas everyone
A fire was lit
S now covered our garden.

Amelia Hall (12)

Teesside High School, Eaglescliffe

Untitled

Snowflakes tumbled from the sky,
A pure white waterfall,
Falling onto the frozen earth.

Footsteps printed in the snow,
Sparkling, icy pools,
Cheerful voices echoing as we go.

Stars lit up the night,
Twinkling lights around the tree.
An abundance of neatly wrapped presents,
All waiting for a happy family.

Ruby Liddle (13)
Teesside High School, Eaglescliffe

Christmas Shopping

In a minute I would see,
Dad had left and abandoned me,
In a shop, all alone,
It felt like an overload.
Picking presents one by one,
My money, almost gone.

After the shops,
Rummaging free,
I felt proud and full of glee.

It was the end of a shopping fight,
Now it's time to say goodnight!

Melanie Dailey (13)
Teesside High School, Eaglescliffe

Untitled

Air wrapped me like a blanket, so cold,
The tree stood luxurious and bold.
Capturing night kept my eye gazing,
The lights on the tree never fading.
Decorated in white snow,
The icy wind started to blow.
The snow fell slowly,
I huddled next to my mum coldly.

Phoebe Dailey (13)
Teesside High School, Eaglescliffe

Candy

C hristmas morning is so fun

A nd when Granny comes she calls you 'hun'

N aughty elf watching over you

D addy is so drunk he has no clue

Y ou have sung and eaten all day, so merry Christmas!

Dominique Moore (12)

Teesside High School, Eaglescliffe

A Christmas Day

We pottered about with endless streams of fairy lights
Soon enough, every surface would be glowing
And the smell of fire filling the air
The roaring fire warmed our toes
As everyone argued over Monopoly.

Harrison Murphy (12)
Teesside High School, Eaglescliffe

Winter Wonderland

The snowflakes are falling
The turkeys are calling
Mothers are crying
Children are laughing
Families are together
But not forever!

Marcus Keenan (13)
Teesside High School, Eaglescliffe

Chaos Christmas

Children happy
Chaos is near
As parents wonder
Why Christmas is here.

Wintertime is here
Advent has started
The countdown has begun
As children wait eagerly.

Children happy
Chaos is near
As parents wonder
Why Christmas is here.

Food is bought
Food is sold
Supermarket sales
Are bold.

Children happy
Chaos is near
As parents wonder
Why Christmas is here.

The tree is up
Everyone helps

As when it is done
It comes falling down.

Children happy
Chaos is near
As parents wonder
Why Christmas is here.

Santa comes down the chimney
His sack is full of presents
Children lie awake
Aware of his presence.

Children happy
Chaos is near
As parents wonder
Why Christmas is here.

The turkey is cooking
Golden brown it is lookin'
Avoiding the sprouts
As they begin to pout.

Children happy
Chaos is near
As parents wonder
Why Christmas is here.

Benjamin Lovell (12)
The Crypt School, Gloucester

The Ivory Festivities

Sleeping quietly, without a sound,
Waiting for the presence of festivities to be achieved.
The snow is bright,
On this soundless night;
The night of Christmas Eve.

Down falls the ivory snow,
Observed as I wake.
I then realised,
And couldn't believe my eyes,
As it was finally Christmas Day.

Walking down the stairs revealed many sights,
Such as an artificial tree decorated with lights.
It was surrounded with tinsel all around,
And I could hear many festive sounds.

Small, wrapped boxes sat under the tree,
Waiting to be shredded apart by me.
Quickly, something crucial had passed:
I had realised that time was flying by, and fast.

After visiting family and friends,
The day was coming to a swift, unwanted end.
Due to this, a meal was served,
The best meal I had ever observed.

The incredible aroma consumed the room,
And the delightful taste occurred when it was consumed.
After a while, the day came to a close,
I then fell asleep, as my eyes were closed.

Jack David Boucher (12)

The Crypt School, Gloucester

A Christmas Cat-Astrophe

As the cat of Christmas went around,
All the kittens were calming down,
Presents, toys and many treats,
All of which were great to eat.

Round and round the cat went,
Until only one house was left which meant...
Oh no, there were no more treats to give out,
He must have dropped one at the roundabout.

Retracing back to where he began,
To find his little kitten's jam.
Phew! He found it at the house named Pam,
But could he get back in time to the house of little Sam?

Leap after leap, step after step,
He finally got back to little Sam's place,
And wow, what perfect timing,
Put it in his stocking and flew away,
Wishing everyone a good Christmas Day.

William Tidmarsh (12)

The Crypt School, Gloucester

The Owl's Watchful Eyes

Children wake up,
Under the tree a surprise.
They're being kept safe,
Under the owl's watchful eyes.

People running around,
Unwrapping their prize.
They're being kept safe,
Under the owl's watchful eyes.

"Get to sleep!
Santa won't come otherwise!"
They're being kept safe,
Under the owl's watchful eyes.

The sharp glance,
Extremely wise.
The piercing gaze,
Of the owl's watchful eyes.

Watching like a hawk,
The guardian angel flies.
Unknown, keeping everyone safe -
The owl's watchful eyes...

Louis Powles (12)
The Crypt School, Gloucester

Superhero Daddy

The jolly presents hide tentatively under the tree,
It's an hour till Xmas, can't you see?
All the beaming faces, crystal clear,
Happy folks laughing hysterically, can't you hear?

Bang! Crash! Wallop! The tree falls over,
My cousin is trapped, it's like an enclosure,
But Superhero Daddy picks it up,
Saving the day, hit him up!

The clock strikes twelve,
Into the chocolate I delve,
It's Christmas time,
And I forgot how to rhyme!

Jack Pryor (12) & Josh
The Crypt School, Gloucester

Christmas Poem

C hristmas time is all about love
H aving fun with all the family
R eindeer flying all over the world
I n everyone's houses, terrible jokes are being told
S anta has delivered all his presents
T rees are sparkling with decorations
M any people are having a great time
A nd no one is left out
S anta's job is complete and successful until next year!

William Robinson (12) & Uzair

The Crypt School, Gloucester

The Jolly Christmas Man

The snow glistened like stars in the clear night sky.
Children cannot get to sleep and everyone knows why.
Through the windows glorious, glittering decorations
you can spy.
Under the tree neatly wrapped presents gleefully lie.
A voice called from the shadows,
"Goodbye jolly fat man, you must die!"
This was accompanied by, "Ho, ho, no!" the children
shall cry.

Jacob Taylor (12)
The Crypt School, Gloucester

Christmas Poem!

Cookies baking in the kitchen,
The smell floats through the air,
We are celebrating Christmas,
With amazing Christmas flair.

We eat our Christmas dinner,
Opening crackers is so fun,
Our Christmas is the best,
It will never be outdone.

This evening they'll sing carols,
With their angel voices,
Our Christmas is amazing,
Which everyone rejoices.

Cameron Frederick (13) & Zac
The Crypt School, Gloucester

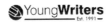

Christmas - Litmas

I am going home for Christmas.
I cannot wait to be home with the family.
Going home to chill with the Bramleys.
Cannot wait to open the presents.
This is a good time for everyone
Even if the rich think you are peasants.
Just sit down and write a letter -
It will make their mouth hum
With a tune of perfect gladness,
If you tell them that you will come.

Oliver Dove (12) & Abdur-Rahman
The Crypt School, Gloucester

Christmas Count

One shining star on top of the tree
Two little children laughing with glee
Three jolly gents standing at the door
Four hungry munchers ask for more
Five Christmas bells, *ring, ring, ring*
Six high voices, sing, sing, sing

It's that wintry time of year
Where choirs sing and bells ring clear,
This is the Christmas count.

Felix Baldwin (13)
The Crypt School, Gloucester

A Christmas Surprise

I once had a Christmas experience,
Oh boy did it stink,
I was hit by a bombardment of droppings,
And it made me think...
I thought and thought and came to the conclusion,
That Santa made a mistake,
I knew from then on that St Nick was not a trick.

Thomas Usmar (12)
The Crypt School, Gloucester